Microblog React Project

Microblog React Project

Cristian Salcescu

ISBN-13: 979-8555900166

History:

November 2020 First Edition

Contents

Preface

This book takes a project-based learning approach by engaging you in building a practical project. The reader will learn things on the way by developing different parts of this application.

Creating this project requires basic JavaScript and React knowledge. For improving your JavaScript skills and functional programming techniques you may consider reading Discover Functional JavaScript and Functional Programming in JavaScript. For an introduction to React concepts from a functional programming perspective take a look at Functional React.

You may use this book as a way to practice what you have learned about React.

The Microblog application will be built using React Hooks, React Rooter, Material UI, Redux, Redux Thunk, Redux Toolkit, and Axios.

When creating the application you are going to encounter challenges like authenticating the user, storing the authorization token and then reuse it for other network calls, displaying a list of items, reading and validating form inputs, adding and deleting items.

Enjoy building the project!

Source Code

The project files from this book are available at
https://github.com/cristi-salcescu/microblog-react.

Feedback

I will be glad to hear your feedback. For comments, questions, or suggestions regarding this book send me an email to cristisalcescu@gmail.com. Thanks in advance for considering to write a review of the book.

Fast Development Environment

The first thing we need to do is to set-up our development environment.

Package Manager

A package manager is a tool used to track project dependencies in an easy to use manner. At the time of writing, Node.js package manager, in short npm, is the most popular. Let's start by installing Node.js.

The following commands can then be used in command prompt to check the Node.js and npm versions:

```
node --version
npm --v
```

NPM Packages

With npm we can install additional packages. These packages are the application dependencies.

For example, here is the command for installing the Redux package:

```
npm install --save redux
```

The installed packages can be found in the node_modules folder. The --save flag tells npm to store the package requirement in the package.json file.

The package.json file stores all the node packages used in the project. These packages are the application dependencies. The application can be shared with other developers without sharing all the node packages.

Installing all the packages defined in the `package.json` file can be done using the `npm install` command.

Create React App

The easiest way to start with a React application is to use Create React App.

To do that, run the following command:

```
npx create-react-app appname
```

`npx` can execute a package that wasn't previously installed.

Once the application is created the following commands can be used:

- `npm start`: starts the development server.
- `npm test`: starts the test runner.
- `npm run build`: builds the app for production into the `build` folder.

IDE

For code editing, we need an Integrated Development Environment, IDE in short.

I am going to use Visual Studio Code but feel free to use any editor you prefer.

To start the application, first, open the application folder in Visual Studio Code. Then open the terminal from Terminal→New Terminal and run: `npm start`. This launches the development server and opens the React application in the browser.

Introduction

When building the microblog application we are going to follow the core functional principles of using pure functions and immutable data.

Immutable objects cannot be changed after creation. Pure functions compute the same result given the same input and have no side-effects. Any interaction with the environment outside the function like changing an external variable, reading, or writing to the HTML DOM, making network calls is a side-effect.

Unidirectional Data Flow

It turns out that the best way to achieve this purity of functions is to put them inside a data flow. Here is a sketch of the unidirectional data flow we are going to follow.

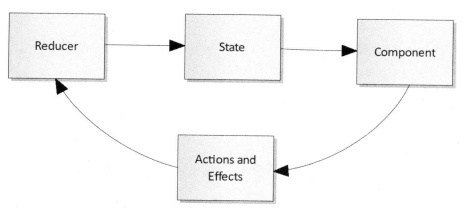

The state defines all the application data that may be displayed on the screen and can change.

The component is a function transforming part of the state data into a visual interface. The visual interface is made of HTML and CSS.

Components define also the actions that are to be dispatched when the user interacts with the UI. I am going to use the word "actions" for synchronous actions and the term "effects" for asynchronous actions.

The plain actions are just data transfer objects describing how the state should change.

The effects are more complex, and we will discuss them on a concrete example. These effects encapsulate impure code and are a compromise we have to do when starting a practical project because there is no popular option for building an application using only pure functions.

The reducer takes the existing state and an action and returns a new state object.

This endless flow where the data is initially stored then displayed on the screen and after that changed based on the user interaction stays at the base of building the application.

In order to implement the previous unidirectional flow, we will use the Redux store. Start by installing the store library.

```
npm install redux react-redux --save
```

Let's examine all these parts on the trivial counter example.

State

In this case, the state is just a number initialized with 0.

```
const initialState = 0;
```

Action Types

We need two action types, one for incrementing the number and the other for decrementing it.

```
const INCREMENT = 'INCREMENT';
const DECREMENT = 'DECREMENT';

export { INCREMENT, DECREMENT };
```

Action Creators

The action creators functions use the previous types to create plain action objects having the **type** property.

```
import { INCREMENT, DECREMENT } from './action-types';

function increment(){
  return {
    type: INCREMENT
  }
}

function decrement(){
  return {
    type: DECREMENT
  }
}

export {
  increment,
  decrement
}
```

Reducer

The reducer function increments the count when the **INCREMENT** action is received and decrements it on the **DECREMENT** action.

```
import { INCREMENT, DECREMENT } from './action-types';

function reducer(counter = initialState, action){
  switch(action.type){
    case INCREMENT:
      return counter + 1;
    case DECREMENT:
      return counter - 1;
    default:
      return counter;
  }
}
```

```
export default reducer;
```

The reducer function should always return the state even if it does not change it. When the reducer does not know how to handle an action it just returns the current input state.

The reducer is a pure function. It has no side-effects. It does not mutate the input state.

Component

The component gets in the counter number and two callbacks, `increment`, and `decrement`. It renders the number and uses the callbacks as click event handlers.

```
import React from 'react';

function Counter({
  counter, increment, decrement }){
   return(
   <div>
     <div>{counter}</div>
     <div>
       <button
         type="button"
         onClick={decrement}>
         -
       </button>
       <button
         type="button"
         onClick={increment}>
         +
       </button>
     </div>
   </div>
   )
}
```

The `Counter` component connects to the store to read the `counter` state and dispatch the `increment` and `decrement` actions.

```
import React from 'react';
import { connect } from 'react-redux';
```

```
import { increment, decrement } from './action-creators';

function Counter({
  counter, increment, decrement}){}

export default connect(
  counter => ({ counter }),
  {increment, decrement}
)(Counter);
```

The connect utility function connects the component to the Redux store. It takes as the first argument a function that extracts data from the store and maps it to the component properties. It accepts as the second argument an object literal mapping action creators to the component property callbacks. When such a callback is called, an action is built using the action creator and then dispatched.

In our case, we extract the whole state and pass it to the component as the `counter` property.

```
counter => ({ counter })
```

Then we map the `increment` and `decrement` action creators to the `increment`, `decrement` property callbacks expected by the `Counter` component. Calling the `increment` callback on the on-click event results in the creation of an action using the `increment` action creator that is then dispatched to the store.

Action Creator Helper

The creation and usage of actions become repetitive. We can simplify their creation using a helper. The Redux Actions library offers such a utility function.

```
npm install redux-actions --save
```

Here is how we can build the action creators using a helper.

```
import { createAction } from 'redux-actions';

const increment = createAction('Increment');
const decrement = createAction('Decrement');
```

```
export default {
  increment,
  decrement
}
```

The `createAction` utility takes a `type` and returns the action creator function. It defines a function that takes a `payload` data object and returns a plain object containing the `type` and the `payload` properties.

```
function createAction(type){
  const actionCreator = payload => ({
    payload,
    type
  });

  return actionCreator;
}
```

In order to get the action type when implicitly using `toString()` on the action creator, we can set the `toString()` method to return that type using Object.defineProperty.

```
function createAction(type){
  const actionCreator = payload => ({
    payload,
    type
  });

  Object.defineProperty(actionCreator, 'toString', {
    value: () => type,
    writable: false
  });

  return actionCreator;
}
```

Let's understand better why we want to have the `toString` method defined on action creators.

Consider the next example.

```
const increment = createAction('Increment');
increment.toString();
//'Increment'
```

`createAction` gets the action type and returns a function.

`increment` is a function. A function is also an object so it has methods. The returned action creator has the `toString` redefined to retrieve the action type. When `increment.toString()` is invoked it gets the `'Increment'` action type.

On an object literal the keys are string only. When using a function as a key, the function is converted to a string using the `toString` method. By setting the `toString` method on action creators to return the action types we can use them as keys on object literals.

Below is an example of creating an object literal mapping the `increment` action creator to the `incrementReducer`. No additional type string constant is required. We can just map directly action creators to the reducer functions.

```
const increment = createAction('Increment');

function incrementReducer(state){
  return state + 1;
}

const map = {
  [increment]: incrementReducer
}
```

The object initializer syntax supports computed property keys. It allows us to put an expression in brackets []. The expression is converted to a string and used as the property key. The `increment` function is converted to a string using the `toString` method and the result, the `'Increment'` string, is used a the property key.

The `map` object can then be used to retrieve the reducer for an action creator.

```
const reducer = map[increment];
reducer(1);
//2
```

We get the same reducer function when using directly the action type string as the key.

```
const reducer = map['Increment'];
reducer(1);
```

//2

Reducer Helper

At this point, the creation of the reducer function can be simplified by using an object mapping action creators to smaller reducer functions.

```
import { handleActions } from 'redux-actions';
import actions from './actions';

const initialState = 0;

function increment(state, action){
  return state + 1;
}

function decrement(state, action){
  return state + 1;
}

export default handleActions({
  [actions.increment]: increment,
  [actions.decrement]: decrement
}, initialState);
```

There are a few advantages to this approach.

First, the code will still be cleaner when we add more logic as the mapping object contains just the matching between the action and the smaller reducer function.

Second, there is no need to keep a distinct piece of information regarding an action: the action creator and the action type. We can map directly the action creator to a smaller updater function.

Third, it forces us to extract out the update logic into a new function with an expressive name.

The handleActions utility that helps us mapping the action to the smaller reducer function may look like the one below.

```
function handleActions(actionMap, initialState){
  return function(state = initialState, action){
    const update = actionMap[action.type];
```

```
    if(typeof(update) === 'function'){
      return update(state, action);
    } else {
      return state;
    }
  }
}
```

The `actionMap` is a map between the action type and the reducer function we have to execute for it.

Redux Toolkit

Redux Toolkit is the recommended approach for working with the Redux store. It includes utilities that simplify common tasks, including the ones discussed before, createAction and createReducer.

`npm install @reduxjs/toolkit --save`

Here is how we can use the `createReducer` helper in a similar way to `handleActions` to simplify the creation of the reducer functions by providing an object mapping actions to smaller reducer functions.

When the specific action is dispatched the associated reducer updates the state.

```
import { createReducer } from '@reduxjs/toolkit';

//...

export default createReducer(initialState, {
    [actions.increment]: increment,
    [actions.decrement]: decrement
  });
```

From now on we are going to use the Redux Toolkit to simplify the action creation and the mapping of actions to smaller reducers.

Knowing all these we can next look at the requirements and start building the application.

Chapter 01: Requirements

The microblog application allows users to connect and create blog posts. They can search and follow other users. When a user is followed all his posts appear on the timeline page.

Timeline

The timeline page displays all the blog posts created by the current user and the posts created by other followed users. Users can delete their own posts.

Timeline

People

Profile

NewPost

Logout

C **How to make complex problems easier**
Our natural way of dealing with complexity is to
break it into smaller pieces and then put everything
back together.

A **Engage all Your Senses When Learning**
Different people like to learn in different ways. Some
prefer reading, others watching training videos, others
learn by doing or by hearing information.

C **Things on null and undefined that you should know**
Null and undefined are the so-called nullish values.
You may know the falsy values which are false, 0,
NaN, empty string '', undefined, and null. So null and
undefined are also falsy values, but they are the only
nullish values.

For each post, the title and the content are shown. On the left side of the post, there is an avatar with the user's initials. On the right, the delete button appears only for the current user posts and allows to remove them.

Profile

The profile page shows the name and email of the user. It also displays the followed users and all the followers. From here the user can decide to follow or unfollow any of these persons.

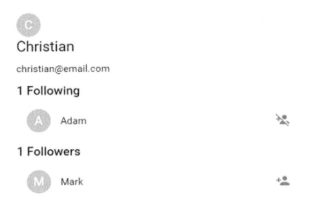

People

The people page allows us to search for other users and to follow or unfollow them.

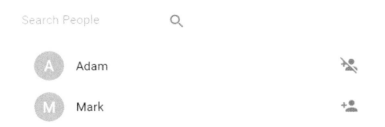

For each person, the full name, the avatar with their initials, and the follow/unfollow button are shown.

Login

The login page is necessary for authenticating the user.

The 'Don't have an account' link navigates to the registration page.

Register

Users that do not have an account can create one from the registration page. All fields are required.

The user can navigate to the login page by pressing the 'Do have an account?' link.

Recap

The microblog application is a social one that allows the user to follow other people and see their short blog posts. The project requires creating an authentication and authorization system.

Chapter 02: API

In order to build the application, we need an API that lets us register and authenticate users, create or read blog posts.

The JSON Server utility allows us to create a fake API. We need to install the json-server-auth module to enable a JWT based authentication flow.

Start by installing the necessary npm modules.

```
npm install -g json-server json-server-auth
```

Users API

The user's API allows registering new users and authenticating the existing ones.

```
POST /register
POST /login
```

Below is an example of the data that we are going to save for a user.

```
[
  {
    "email": "christian@email.com",
    "password": "$xxx...",
    "name": "Christian",
    "id": 1
  },
  {
    "email": "adam@email.com",
    "password": "$xxx...",
    "name": "Adam",
    "id": 2
  }
```

```
]
```

Both the login and registration APIs return a response containing a JWT access token that expires in one hour.

```
{
  "accessToken": "xxx.xxx.xxx"
}
```

Posts API

The posts API permits to create, delete, and get posts.

```
POST    /posts
DELETE  /posts/1
GET     /posts
```

Here is an example of a few blog posts.

```
[
  {
    "title": "How to make ...",
    "content": "Our natural way ...",
    "userId": 1,
    "userName": "Christian",
    "id": 1
  },
  {
    "title": "Engage all ...",
    "content": "Different people ...",
    "userId": 2,
    "userName": "Adam",
    "id": 2
  }
]
```

As an example, in order to read all the blog posts created by the users with the ids 1 and 2 we should make the following GET call.

```
GET /posts?userId=1&userId=2
```

Followers API

The followers API enables to add or delete followers.

```
POST    /followers
DELETE /followers/1
```

Below is an example of how this relational data looks like.

```
[
  {
    "userId": 2,
    "followerId": 1,
    "id": 1
  },
  {
    "userId": 1,
    "followerId": 3,
    "id": 2
  }
]
```

The `userId` stores the id of the followed user and `followerId` keeps the follower's id. Each row keeps a relation between these two users and can be deleted only using the relation id.

Security

The json-server-auth module allows securing the APIs.

For example, it creates a route `/660/posts` that can be accessed only by logged users. We can then use the custom routes feature to secure the access to the direct routes.

Create a `routes.json` file with the following routes.

```
{
  "/users*": "/660/users$1",
  "/posts*": "/660/posts$1",
  "/followers*": "/660/followers$1"
}
```

At this point, the users API, posts API and followers API can only be accessed by providing in the request header the token retrieved from the login or the registration APIs.

Run the following command to start the fake API.

```
json-server-auth db.json --watch db.json -p 3001 -r routes.json
```

Recap

JSON Server lets us to build a fake API on the fly by just creating a JSON file with the sample data.

The additional JSON Server Auth module enables a simple JWT based authentication flow.

Chapter 03: Components

Our natural way of building a complex interface is to split it into parts. These parts are called components and in React they can be expressed using just functions.

Next, we are going to define all the components that create the UI. The interface will be based on the Material UI basic components.

Start by installing the library.

```
npm install @material-ui/core --save
```

Timeline

The `Timeline` component is a function that takes a list of blog posts and creates the HTML representation of it.

How to make complex problems easier
Our natural way of dealing with complexity is to break it into smaller pieces and then put everything back together.

Engage all Your Senses When Learning
Different people like to learn in different ways. Some prefer reading, others watching training videos, others learn by doing or by hearing information.

Things on null and undefined that you should know
Null and undefined are the so-called nullish values. You may know the falsy values which are false, 0, NaN, empty string '', undefined, and null. So null and undefined are also falsy values, but they are the only nullish values.

We start by importing the necessary component from the Material UI library.

```
import React from 'react';

import List from
  '@material-ui/core/List';
import ListItem from
  '@material-ui/core/ListItem';
import Divider from
```

```
  '@material-ui/core/Divider';
import ListItemText from
  '@material-ui/core/ListItemText';
import ListItemAvatar from
  '@material-ui/core/ListItemAvatar';
import Avatar from
  '@material-ui/core/Avatar';
import ListItemSecondaryAction from
  '@material-ui/core/ListItemSecondaryAction';
import IconButton from
  '@material-ui/core/IconButton';
import DeleteIcon from
  '@material-ui/icons/Delete';
```

The `Timeline` component wraps the blog post list inside the Material UI List component. Then it maps each post to a ListItem component.

```
function Timeline({ posts }) {
  return (
  <List>
  {
    posts.map(post => (
      <React.Fragment key={post.id}>
        <ListItem>
        <!-- ... -->
        </ListItem>
        <Divider />
      </React.Fragment>
    ))
  }
  </List>
  );
}
```

```
export default Timeline;
```

Keys uniquely identifies a list item. We are using `post.id` to give it a stable unique identity.

The items in the list are divided with a Divider. Dividers can be used to separate content in lists. Because we actually used two elements for each item, `ListItem` and `Divider`, we have to wrap them inside a single element. React.Fragment helps us to do that by grouping several elements without adding extra nodes to the DOM. There is also a syntactic sugar for it <></>.

Inside the list item, the ListItemAvatar component shows an avatar with the user initials. The ListItemText component displays text in a list item. In our case, it shows the `title` and the `content` of a blog post.

```
<ListItem alignItems="flex-start" >
  <ListItemAvatar>
    <Avatar alt={post.userName}>
      {getAvatarTitle(post.userName)}
    </Avatar>
  </ListItemAvatar>
  <ListItemText
    primary={post.title}
    secondary={post.content}
  />
  <ListItemSecondaryAction>
    <IconButton>
      <DeleteIcon />
    </IconButton>
  </ListItemSecondaryAction>
</ListItem>
```

The delete button is wrapped inside the `ListItemSecondaryAction` component to be shown as a secondary action.

The `getAvatarTitle` function takes a full name and retrieves the initials.

```
function getAvatarTitle(fullName){
  const names = fullName.split(' ');
  const letters =
    names.map(name => name.charAt(0));

  return letters.join('');
}
```

Here is the result of calling it with a full name.

```
getAvatarTitle('Niall Ferguson');
//'NF'
```

The full name 'Niall Ferguson' is split into an array of strings

['Niall', 'Ferguson']. Then we map over each name and extract the first letter ['N', 'F']. In the end, all these letters are joined in a string that is returned as the result.

Root Component

We can start trying out these components by rendering them inside the App root component.

The Timeline component expects a list of blog posts. We can hardcode such a list and then pass it to the component.

```
import React from 'react';

import Container from
  '@material-ui/core/Container';
import Timeline from './posts/Timeline';

const posts = [
  {
    "title": "How to make ...",
    "content": "Our natural way ...",
    "userId": 1,
    "userName": "Christian",
    "id": 1
  },
  //...
]

function App() {
  return (
    <Container>
      <Timeline posts={posts} />
    </Container>
  );
}

export default App;
```

The Container component centers the content horizontally.

Entry Point

In the application entry point, the `index.js` file, the `App` component is rendered on the screen.

```
import React from 'react';
import ReactDOM from 'react-dom';
import App from './App';

ReactDOM.render(
  <React.StrictMode>
    <App />
  </React.StrictMode>,
  document.getElementById('root')
);
```

New Post

The `NewPost` form component lets the user add a new post.

```
function NewPost({ addPost }) {
    return <form></form>
}
```

Form input elements have an associated state. For each input, we declare the associated state using the useState hook.

The `useState` hook returns the current state and a function that updates it.

```
const [title, setTitle] = useState('');
```

`title` gives access to the current state and `setTitle` lets us modifying it. Then we associate the title text input with this state. The text field reads the state using the `value` property and changes the state using the `onChange` event. An input with both the value and the `onChange` property set is called a controlled input.

```
<TextField
 name="title"
 value={title}
 onChange={e => setTitle(e.target.value)}
/>
```

When the post button is clicked the `submitForm` handler is called.

```
<Button
 onClick={submitForm} >
   Post
</Button>
```

The `submitForm` function creates a new post data object using the information from the state variables. Then it invokes the `addPost` callback with this newly created object.

```
function submitForm(){
  const post = {
    title,
    content
  };

  addPost(post);
}
```

The `NewPost` component receives the `addPost` callback and invokes it with a new post data when the post button is clicked. Callback properties are used to send data to parent components.

Here is the full component code.

```
import React, {useState} from 'react';
import Box from
  '@material-ui/core/Box';
import FormControl from
  '@material-ui/core/FormControl';
import FormGroup from
  '@material-ui/core/FormGroup';
import TextField from
  '@material-ui/core/TextField';
import Button from
  '@material-ui/core/Button';

function NewPost({ addPost }) {

  const [title, setTitle] = useState('');
  const [content, setContent] = useState('');

  function submitForm(){
    const post = {
```

```
      title,
      content
    };

    addPost(post);
  }

  return (
  <form>
    <FormGroup>
      <FormControl>
        <TextField
          label="Title"
          name="title"
          value={title}
          onChange={e=>setTitle(e.target.value)}
        />
      </FormControl>
    </FormGroup>

    <FormGroup>
      <TextField
        label="Share your thoughts"
        name="content"
        value={content}
        onChange={e=>setContent(e.target.value)}
        multiline
        rows={4}
      />
    </FormGroup>

    <Box mt={1}>
      <Button
        variant="contained"
        color="primary"
        onClick={submitForm} >
          Post
      </Button>
    </Box>
  </form>
```

```
    );
}
```

```
export default NewPost;
```

Again, we can test it out by importing and rendering it in the **App** root component.

```
import React from 'react';

import Container from
  '@material-ui/core/Container';
import NewPost from './posts/NewPost';

function App() {
  return (
    <Container>
      <NewPost addPost={console.log} />
    </Container>
  );
}
```

```
export default App;
```

People

The `People` component displays a list of people. The `Profile` component renders a similar list twice, one for the followed people and the other for the followers.

Instead of repeating the rendering logic three times, we can create the `PeopleList` component and reuse it in all these places.

First we import the necessary components from the Material UI library.

```
import React from 'react';

import List from
  '@material-ui/core/List';
import ListItem from
  '@material-ui/core/ListItem';
import ListItemText from
  '@material-ui/core/ListItemText';
```

```
import ListItemAvatar from
  '@material-ui/core/ListItemAvatar';
import Avatar from
  '@material-ui/core/Avatar';
import ListItemSecondaryAction from
  '@material-ui/core/ListItemSecondaryAction';
import IconButton from
  '@material-ui/core/IconButton';
import PersonAddIcon from
  '@material-ui/icons/PersonAdd';
import PersonAddDisabledIcon from
  '@material-ui/icons/PersonAddDisabled';
```

The PeopleList gets a list of people and transforms into a visual interface. When the user clicks the follow button it calls the follow callback. Similarly, when the user clicks the unfollow button it calls the unfollow callback.

```
import { getAvatarTitle } from '../user/utils.js';

function PeopleList({
  people, follow, unfollow}) {

return (
  <List>
  {
    people.map(user => (
      <ListItem key={user.id}>
        <ListItemAvatar>
        <Avatar alt={user.name}>
          {getAvatarTitle(user.name)}
        </Avatar>
        </ListItemAvatar>
        <ListItemText
         primary={user.name}
        />
        <ListItemSecondaryAction>
          <IconButton
          onClick={() => unfollow(user.id)}>
          <PersonAddDisabledIcon />
          </IconButton>
```

```
            <IconButton
              onClick={() => follow(user.id)}>
              <PersonAddIcon />
            </IconButton>
          </ListItemSecondaryAction>
        </ListItem>
    ))
  }
  </List>
  );
}


export default PeopleList;
```

The PeopleSearch component lets users search for a specific text.

```
import React, { useState } from 'react';

import InputBase from
  '@material-ui/core/InputBase';
import IconButton from
  '@material-ui/core/IconButton';
import SearchIcon from
  '@material-ui/icons/Search';

function PeopleSearch({ onSearch }) {

  const [text, setText] = useState('')

  return (
  <form>
    <InputBase
      placeholder="Search People"
      value={text}
      onChange={e=>setText(e.target.value)}
      autoFocus
    />

    <IconButton onClick={()=>onSearch(text)}>
      <SearchIcon />
    </IconButton>
```

```
        </form>
    );
}
```

```
export default PeopleSearch;
```

PeopleSearch is a simple component with a textbox and a button. The textbox has an associated state. The search input is a controlled input, it has both the `value` and the `onChange` properties set.

When the search button is clicked the `onSearch` callback is invoked with the new search text.

People

The `People` component can be built using the previous `PeopleList` and `PeopleSearch` components.

```
import React from 'react';
```

```
import PeopleSearch from './PeopleSearch';
import PeopleList from './PeopleList';
```

```
function People({ people }) {
    return (
    <React.Fragment>
      <PeopleSearch
       onSearch={console.log} />

      <PeopleList
       people={people} />
    </React.Fragment>
    );
}
```

```
export default People;
```

The `People` takes a list of people and sends it to the `PeopleList` component. For the moment, it handles the `onSearch` event on the `PeopleSearch` component by displaying the search text in the console.

Profile

The `Profile` component takes in the user data and displays it on screen.

It also renders the list of followed users and the list of followers using the `PeopleList` component.

```
import React from 'react';

import Avatar from
  '@material-ui/core/Avatar';
import Typography from
  '@material-ui/core/Typography';

import PeopleList from './PeopleList';
import { getAvatarTitle } from
  '../user/utils.js';

function Profile({ user, followingList, followersList }) {
  return (
  <React.Fragment>
    <Avatar alt={user.name}>
      {getAvatarTitle(user.name)}
    </Avatar>
    <Typography variant="h5" gutterBottom>
      {user.name}
    </Typography>
    <Typography variant="subtitle1" gutterBottom>
      {user.email}
    </Typography>

    <Typography variant="h6" >
      {followingList.length} Following
    </Typography>
    <PeopleList
     people={followingList} />

    <Typography variant="h6" >
    {followersList.length} Followers
    </Typography>

    <PeopleList
```

```
      people={followersList} />
    </React.Fragment>
  );
}
```

```
export default Profile;
```

The Typography component is a way of standardizing the categories of text. We don't have to add a `<div>` with a `className` to set specific styles.

Recap

Our main technique for creating the UI is to split it into small parts called components and then develop and combine them.

Components are actually functions that received plain data objects and callbacks as inputs. Plain data objects are used to take data in and transform it into HTML and CSS. Callbacks are used to send data out on user interactions.

When we look back at these components we can notice that ones that have no state, the stateless components like `Timeline`, `PeopleList`, or `Profile` are pure functions. The stateful components like `NewPost` and `PeopleSearch` are impure.

Chapter 04: Validation

In this chapter, we will create the login and registration forms. Both of them require validation so we are going to implement a customizable validation system that can be used in other forms.

Login

Start with the login page. It lets users enter their credentials.

```
function Login({ login }) {

  const [email, setEmail] = useState('');
  const [password, setPassword] = useState('');

  return (...)
}


export default Login;
```

The email and password inputs require an associated state. For both of them, we define the state using the `useState` hook.

When the email text field is rendered it takes the current state value in the `value` property. When the input text changes the `setEmail` function is called with the new input value. The same thing happens for the password text field. The two inputs are defined using the `TextField` Material UI component.

```
<TextField
 value={email}
 onChange={e => setEmail(e.target.value)}
/>
```

```
<TextField
 value={password}
 onChange={e => setPassword(e.target.value)}
/>
```

When the user clicks the login button the `submitForm` function is invoked.

```
<Button
  color="primary"
  onClick={submitForm}>
  Login
</Button>
```

The `Login` component takes as input the `login` callback. When the login button is clicked the `submitForm` creates a new data object using the state variables and invokes the `login` callback with this object.

```
function Login({ login }) {
  function submitForm(){
    const credentials = { email, password };
    login(credentials);
  }

  return ()
}
```

Now let's display the validation messages for the required inputs.

We need to store the errors as state information.

```
const [errors, setErrors] = useState({});
```

Submitting the form invokes the validation system and if it fails the error messages are displayed on the screen.

```
function Login({ login }) {

  const [email, setEmail] = useState('');
  const [password, setPassword] = useState('');
  const [errors, setErrors] = useState({});

  function validate(){
    let emailError = '';
    let passwordError = '';
    let isValid = true;
```

```
  if(email === ''){
    emailError = 'Field is required';
    isValid = false;
  }

  if(password === ''){
    passwordError = 'Field is required';
    isValid = false;
  }

  return {
    isValid,
    errors : {
      email: emailError,
      password: passwordError
    }
  }
}

function submitForm(){}

return (
<Container maxWidth="xs">
<form>
  <TextField
   value={email}
   onChange={e=>setEmail(e.target.value)}
   required
   error = {!!errors.email}
   helperText={errors.email}
  />

  <TextField
   type="password"
   value={password}
   onChange={e=>setPassword(e.target.value)}
   required
   error = {!!errors.password}
   helperText={errors.password}
```

```
      />

      <Button
       onClick={submitForm}>
        Login
      </Button>
    </form>
   </Container>
   );
}
```

```
export default Login;
```

When the `error` property of the text filed is set to `true` the input appears with a red border. The `helperText` displays the error message.

Note the use of `!!` before the error message.

```
<TextField error = {!!errors.password} />
```

The `error` property accepts only a boolean. The `!!` before the text string transforms it into a boolean. When the error message is empty it evaluates to `false`. When the text is not empty it evaluates to `true`.

We can get the same result using the built-in `Boolean` function.

```
<TextField error = {Boolean(errors.password)} />
```

The `validate` function returns a boolean indicating if the validation succeeded or not, plus an object with all the error messages.

The `submitForm` function calls the `validate` function validating the form. When the form is valid it just invokes the `login` callback with the new credentials data. When the validation fails it updates the `errors` state variable with the new error messages. Changing the state implies rerendering the component and showing the new error messages on the screen.

```
function submitForm(){
   const { isValid, errors } = validate();

   if(isValid){
     const credentials = { email, password };
     login(credentials);
   } else {
     setErrors(errors);
```

```
  }
}
```

Custom Validation Hook

We are going to create a custom hook that encapsulates the validation system. Each input element will have an associated value and error.

A custom hook is a function whose name begins with "use" and may call other hooks.

The custom hook gives us access to four items. It does that by returning an array with four elements.

```
import { useState } from 'react';

function useFormState(initialValue){
  const [state, setState] = useState(initialValue);

  function setValueFromEvent(e){}
  function validate(){}
  function resetForm(){}

  return [
    state,
    setValueFromEvent,
    validate,
    resetForm
  ];
}

export { useFormState };
```

The component using the useFormState hook will be able to access all these items using the destructuring syntax.

```
const [
    state,
    setValueFromEvent,
    validate,
    resetForm
  ] = useFormState({});
```

The `state` variable lets us read the current state. Here is how the initial state may look like.

```
{
  name: {
    value: '',
    required: true
  },
  email: {
    value: '',
    required: true
  }
}
```

For each input, it contains the current `value` and all the necessary validations. In our case, we support only the `required` validation.

The `setValueFromEvent` allows us to change the state. `setValueFromEvent` works as a callback for the `onChange` event. It extracts the input's `name` and `value` from the event and modifies the state. The input using it should have the `name` attribute defined.

```
function setValueFromEvent(e){
    const { value, name } = e.target;

    const input = state[name];
    const error = validateInput(input, value);

    setState({
      ...state,
      [name] : {
        ...input,
        value,
        error
      }
    });
  }
```

`setValueFromEvent` updates the current `value` of the input in the state variable. It also changes the error message. In case of an error, the state may look like this.

```
  {
```

```
    email: {
      value: '',
      error: 'Field is required'
    },
    password: {
      value: '',
      error: 'Field is required'
    }
  }
```

Here is how the state may look when validations have passed.

```
  {
    email: {
      value: 'christian@email.com',
      error: ''
    },
    password: {
      value: 'password',
      error: ''
    }
  }
```

The `validateInput` function gets the input data object containing all the validation for a specific property and the current value of that property. It checks if the current value meets all the validation criteria and returns an error message. When all validations have passed it returns an empty string. At the moment the `validateInput` supports only the `required` validation, but it can be extended later.

```
  function validateInput(input, value){
    let error = '';

    if(input.required && value === ''){
      error = 'Field is required';
    }

    return error;
  }
```

`validate` validates all the inputs' values and updates the state with the error messages. It returns `true` when the validation succeeds.

```
function validate(){
  const newState = {};
  Object.entries(state).forEach(([name, input]) => {
      const error = validateInput(input, input.value);

      newState[name] = {
          ...input,
          error
      }
  });

  setState(newState);

  const isValid = Object
    .values(newState)
    .every(input => input.error === '');

  return isValid;
}
```

Object.entries() allows us to get all the properties of an object as an array of [key, value] pairs. Once we have that we can iterate over it using the forEach array method. We validate all properties using the validateInput function and create a new state object containing the error messages for all properties. After the newState object is created it used to update the current state. In the end, we use the Object.values() to retrieve all input objects and detect if there is any error. The every array method returns true when all properties have no errors, meaning the error messages are empty strings. When an error message is found, the every method stops and returns false.

resetForm resets the form's inputs to their initial values.

```
function resetForm(){
  setState(initialValue);
}
```

Register

The register page enables us to create a new user.

Let's use the useFormState hook to build the state required for the registration form.

```
import React, { useState } from 'react';
...
import {useFormState} from '../shared/useFormState';

function Register({ registerUser }) {

  const [state, setInputValue, validate] = useFormState({
    name :{
      value: '',
      required: true
    },
    email: {
      value: '',
      required: true
    },
    password: {
      value: '',
      required: true
    }
  });

  return (...);
}

export default Register;
```

The useFormState hook requires to create all the form inputs as properties in the initialization object. For each input we must define the initial value and the validators. At the moment, the custom hook supports only the required validator.

The submit function uses the validate function returned by the useFormState hook to validate the form. When the validation succeeds it builds a plain registration object using the state variable and invokes the registerUser callback with it.

```
function submit(){
  if(validate()){
    const user = {
      name: state.name.value,
      email: state.email.value,
      password: state.password.value
```

```
    };
    registerUser(user);
  }
}
```

The `Register` component takes the `registerUser` callback in props. When the create button is clicked the `submit` function is invoked calling the `registerUser` callback with the registration data.

```
<Button
  variant="contained"
  color="primary"
  onClick={submit}>
  Register
</Button>
```

The text fields read the data from the state using the `value` property. The `onChange` property is set to the `setInputValue` function that updates the form state. The `error` property marking the red border is read from the associated state property. The `helperText` property is used for rendering the validation message. These properties are set for all three text inputs: name, email, and password.

```
<Container maxWidth="xs">
  <div>
    <Typography
      component="h4"
    variant="h4">
      Register
    </Typography>
    <form>
    <FormGroup>
      <FormControl margin="normal">
      <TextField
        variant="outlined"
        label="Name"
        name="name"
        value={state.name.value}
        onChange={setInputValue}
        error={!!state.name.error}
        helperText={state.name.error}
        required
```

```
        />
      </FormControl>
    </FormGroup>
    <FormGroup>
      <FormControl margin="normal">
      <TextField
        variant="outlined"
        label="Email"
        name="email"
        value={state.email.value}
        onChange={setInputValue}
        error={!!state.email.error}
        helperText={state.email.error}
        required
      />
    </FormControl>
    </FormGroup>
    <FormGroup>
      <FormControl margin="normal">
        <TextField
          variant="outlined"
          label="Password"
          name="password"
          type="password"
          value={state.password.value}
          onChange={setInputValue}
          error={!!state.password.error}
          helperText={state.password.error}
        />
    </FormControl>
    </FormGroup>
    </form>
  </div>
</Container>
```

New Post

In a similar way, we can enable the validation system in the NewPost
component. The form has two inputs, the title and the content. Both are
required.

The useFormState custom hook defines the associated state for this form. It contains a property for each field. Both fields are marked as required and initialized with an empty string.

```
import React from 'react';
import Box from
  '@material-ui/core/Box';
import FormControl from
  '@material-ui/core/FormControl';
import FormGroup from
  '@material-ui/core/FormGroup';
import TextField from
  '@material-ui/core/TextField';
import Button from
  '@material-ui/core/Button';

import { useFormState } from '../shared/useFormState';

function NewPost({ addPost }) {
  const [state, setInputValue, validate] =
    useFormState({
      title :{
        value: '',
        required: true
      },
      content: {
        value: '',
        required: true
      }
    });

  function submitForm(){ ... }

  return (
  <form>
    <FormGroup>
      <FormControl>
        <TextField
          label="Title"
          name="title"
          value={state.title.value}
```

```
              onChange={setInputValue}
              error={!!state.title.error}
              helperText={state.title.error}
              />
          </FormControl>
        </FormGroup>

        <FormGroup>
          <TextField
            label="Share your thoughts"
            name="content"
            value={state.content.value}
            onChange={setInputValue}
            error={!!state.content.error}
            helperText={state.content.error}
            multiline
            rows={4}
          />
        </FormGroup>

        <Box mt={1}>
          <Button
            variant="contained"
            color="primary"
            onClick={submitForm} >
              Post
          </Button>
        </Box>
      </form>
    );
}


export default NewPost;
```

Again notice how the state variable is used to set properties on the TextField component.

```
<TextField
 value={state.title.value}
 onChange={setInputValue}
 error={!!state.title.error}
```

```
helperText={state.title.error}
/>
```

The `submitForm` function is called when the post button is clicked. It validates the form and invokes the `addPost` callback only when the validation succeeds.

```
function submitForm(){
  if(validate()){
     const post = {
     title : state.title.value,
     content: state.content.value
   };

   addPost(post);
  }
}
```

Recap

Form validation requires storing the error message associated with each field.

The validation system can be encapsulated inside a custom hook that is initialized with the required validators for each input.

Chapter 05: Routing

In this chapter, we are going to enable a routing system that lets us navigate between pages using the React Router.

Start by installing the library.

```
npm install react-router-dom --save
```

Routes

Inside the App root component, define all the routes.

All router components have to be wrapped inside the BrowserRouter component. Then each new route is defined using Route component. The component attribute of the route defines the component to render when the path matches.

```
import React from 'react';
import { BrowserRouter as Router, Route, Switch }
    from 'react-router-dom';

import Container from
    '@material-ui/core/Container';
import Grid from
    '@material-ui/core/Grid';
import Menu from './Menu';
import NewPost from './posts/NewPost';
import Timeline from './posts/Timeline';
import People from './people/People';
import Profile from './people/Profile';
import Login from './user/Login';
import Register from './user/Register';
```

```
const posts = [
  //...
];

const people = [
  //...
];

const user = people[0];

function App() {
  return (
  <Router>
    <Route
     exact
     path={['/', '/people', '/profile', '/newpost']}>
      <Container>
      <Grid container spacing={1}>
        <Grid item md={3} xs={12} lg={2}>
          <Menu />
        </Grid>
        <Grid item md={6} xs={12} lg={4}>
        <Switch>
          <Route
           path="/"
           exact
           component={() =>
            <Timeline posts={posts} />} />
          <Route
           path="/people"
           component={() =>
            <People people={people} />} />
          <Route
           path="/profile"
           component={() =>
             <Profile
              user={user}
              followingList={people}
              followersList={people} />
            } />
```

```
          <Route
           path='/newpost'
           component={NewPost} />
          </Switch>
        </Grid>
      </Grid>
      </Container>
    </Route>
    <Route
     path={["/register", "/login"]}>
      <Route
        path="/register"
        component={Register} />
      <Route
        path="/login"
        component={Login} />
    </Route>
  </Router>
  );
}
```

```
export default App;
```

When the / route is accessed the `Timeline` component is displayed.

When the `/people` route is accessed the `People` component is displayed.

The `Profile` component is shown when the user navigates to the `/profile` route.

We haven't implemented the logic associate with these components so for the moment we need to send hardcoded data to them. The standard approach of setting the `component` property to an actual component doesn't allow us to pass in extra properties.

```
<Route
 path='/people'
 component={People}
/>
```

An alternative option that supports sending additional data to the component is to use a function that creates the React element.

```
<Route
```

```
 path='/people'
 component={() =>
   <People people={people} />}
/>
```

The Material UI Grid allows us to create a responsive 12-column grid layout. In our case, a menu is always displayed on the left for all routes except the security ones. For the **/register** and **/login** routes no menu is displayed.

Menu

Next, we will create a side menu that enables us to navigate to these routes.

The menu is created using the MenuItem components wrapped inside the MenuList component.

The Link router component makes it possible to navigate to a specific route in the application.

```
import React from 'react';
import MenuItem from
  '@material-ui/core/MenuItem';
import MenuList from
  '@material-ui/core/MenuList';
import { Link } from 'react-router-dom';

function BlogMenuList({ logout}) {
  return (
  <MenuList>
    <MenuItem
      component={Link}
      to='/'>
      Timeline
    </MenuItem>
    <MenuItem
      component={Link}
      to='/people'>
      People
    </MenuItem>
    <MenuItem
      component={Link}
```

```
      to='/profile'>
      Profile
    </MenuItem>
    <MenuItem
      component={Link}
      to="/newpost">
      NewPost
    </MenuItem>
    <MenuItem onClick={logout}>
      Logout
    </MenuItem>
  </MenuList>
  );
}
```

```
export default BlogMenuList;
```

By default menu items are rendered as `<li>` HTML elements. Their `component` property lets us render them as router `Link` components.

Recap

The routing system enables navigation between pages.

The `App` root component defines all the navigation routes. A left-side menu allowing to navigate to these routes is displayed for all pages except the ones authenticating and registering the user.

Chapter 06: Authentication

In this chapter, we are going to add behavior to the application starting with the authentication system.

Begin by installing the necessary libraries.

```
npm install redux react-redux @reduxjs/toolkit --save
npm install axios --save
```

API

Axios is an easy to use promise-based library used to make HTTP requests.

A promise is an object that gives access to a future result of asynchronous operations like a network call. Asynchronous calls provide a way of getting data from Web APIs without blocking the interface.

Create an `api.js` file to encapsulate all the network requests necessary for the required functionality. All functions doing API calls return promises.

The `registerUser` function creates a new user by posting the user data object to the `/regiter` API.

```
import axios from 'axios';

const baseUrl = 'http://localhost:3001';

function registerUser(data){
  return axios
    .post(`${baseUrl}/register`, data)
    .then(getData);
}

function getData(response){
```

```
    return response.data;
}

export default {
  registerUser
};
```

The `login` function authenticates the user by posting its credentials to the `/login` API.

```
function login(data){
  return axios
    .post(`${baseUrl}/login`, data)
    .then(getData);
}
```

Once the user is authenticated and we received the JWT token we need to make another call to take additional data about the user like its name and email. The `fetchUser` function does just that. The `/users` API is a secured one. We need to send a valid token along with the request to have access to it.

```
function fetchUser(email, token){
  return axios
    .get(`${baseUrl}/users?email=${email}`,
      header(token))
    .then(getData)
    .then(getFirst);
}

function getFirst(arr){
  return arr[0];
}
```

Notice how we are using the promise chaining system to create a pipeline. The result of the fetch request is sent as input to the `getData` function that extracts the `data` property from it. Then the returned result, which is an array in our case, is sent to the `getFirst` function that extracts the first element from this array. The returned result of the `fetchUser` function is a promise that when is resolved contains the first element of the returned array from the `/users` API.

The `header` function builds the authorization header with the required token.

```
function header(token){
  return {
    headers: {
      authorization: `Bearer ${token}`
    }
  };
}
```

Next, we will create all the parts involved in the unidirectional data flow implemented using the Redux store. Remember the sketch of the flow.

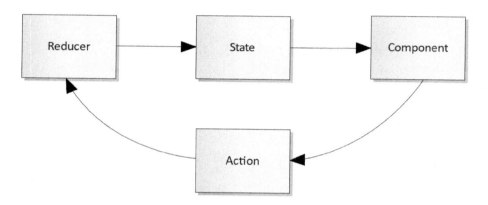

State

State is data that is stored and can be changed.

What data do we need to store in regards to the authenticated user? We need to store his email, his name, the authorization token, and a boolean indicating if the user has been authenticated.

```
const initialState = {
  token: '',
  id: 0,
  name: '',
  email: '',
  authenticated : false
}
```

Actions

Actions are needed to update the store. We need to update the JWT token and the current user data. We also have to clear all this data when the user logs-out.

```
import { createAction } from '@reduxjs/toolkit';

const SetToken = createAction('SetToken');
const SetUser = createAction('SetUser');
const Logout = createAction('Logout');

export default {
  SetToken,
  SetUser,
  Logout
};
```

Effects

Any interaction with the outside environment, like a network request, is a side-effect.

We are going to use the term "effects" for these functions encapsulating side-effects and dispatching plain actions for state changes. The effects will be implemented using the Redux-Thunk middleware for Redux.

The `login` effect makes the API call to authenticate the user and gets back the JWT token. It saves this token in the store by dispatching an action. It then retrieves all the user data by dispatching the `fetchUser` effect. After that, it redirects the user to the timeline page.

```
import api from './api';
import actions from './actions';

function login(credentials){
  return function(dispatch){
    return api.login(credentials)
      .then(actions.SetToken)
      .then(dispatch)
      .then(()=>fetchUser(credentials.email))
      .then(dispatch)
      .then(redirectToTimeline)
```

```
    }
}
```

```
function redirectToTimeline(){
  window.location.replace('/');
}
```

Note how all these functions are executed in a pipeline.

The `registerUser` effect makes the API call to create the user and receives the JWT token. It then dispatches an action to update the state with the new value. After that, it redirects the user to the timeline page.

```
function registerUser(user){
  return function(dispatch){
    return api.registerUser(user)
      .then(actions.SetToken)
      .then(dispatch)
      .then(()=>fetchUser(user.email))
      .then(dispatch)
      .then(redirectToTimeline);
  }
}
```

The `logout` effect dispatches the `Logout` action and redirects the user to the login page.

```
function logout(){
  return function(dispatch){
    Promise.resolve()
      .then(actions.Logout)
      .then(dispatch)
      .then(redirectToLogin)
  }
}
```

```
function redirectToLogin(){
  window.location.replace('/login');
}
```

Promise.resolve creates a resolved promise on the fly. This promise is then used to create a pipeline.

The `fetchUser` effect reads the email and token of the current user from the store and makes a network call to retrieve more pieces of information about the user. Then it builds and dispatches the `SetUser` action to update the state. Effects have access to the current state via the `getState` function.

```
function fetchUser(email){
  return function(dispatch, getState){
    const state = getState();
    const { token } = state.user;

    return api.fetchUser(email, token)
      .then(actions.SetUser)
      .then(dispatch)
  }
}
```

All the effects are exported.

```
export default {
  registerUser,
  login,
  logout
};
```

Reducer

The reducer is the name given to a pure function used to update the state.

When the `SetToken` action is received the state is updated with the new value.

When the `SetUser` action is received the current user is updated.

When the `Logout` action is received the current user and token are cleared.

```
import { createReducer } from '@reduxjs/toolkit';
import actions from './actions';

function setToken(state, action){
  const token = action.payload.accessToken;
  return {
    ...state,
    token,
    authenticated : true
```

```
  };
}

function setUser(state, action){
  const user = action.payload;
  return {
    ...state,
    ...user
  };
}

function logout(){
  return initialState;
}

export default createReducer(initialState, {
  [actions.SetToken]: setToken,
  [actions.SetUser]: setUser,
  [actions.Logout]: logout
});
```

Root Reducer

The root reducer should delegate the management of the user state branch to the new reducer.

```
import { combineReducers } from 'redux';
import user from './user/reducer';

export default combineReducers({
  user
});
```

Login Component

The Login component needs to be connected to the store to dispatch the login effect.

```
import { connect } from 'react-redux';
import effects from './effects';

function Login({ login }) {
```

```
  //...
}

export default connect(
  null, {
  ...effects
}
)(Login);
```

The connect utility connects a component to the store and gives it access to read the state data and dispatch plain actions and effects.

By using the spread syntax to pass effects as the second argument to the connect utility we give access to the component to all the defined effects.

Below is a sketch showing the of unirectional flow when components dispatch effects.

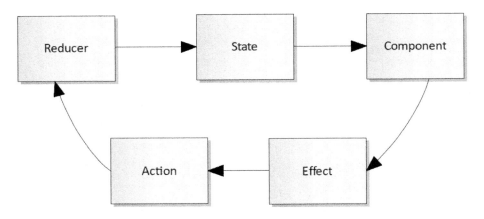

Register Component

The Register component has to be connected to the store. It dispatches the registerUser effect when the registerUser callback is invoked.

```
import { connect } from 'react-redux';
import effects from './effects';

function Register({ registerUser }) {
  //...
}
```

```
export default connect(
  null, {
  ...effects
}
)(Register);
```

Logout

The `BlogMenuList` component must be connected to the store in order to dispatch the `logout` effect.

```
import { connect } from 'react-redux';
import effects from './user/effects';

function BlogMenuList({ logout}) {
  //...
}

export default connect(
  null, {
  ...effects
}
)(BlogMenuList);
```

Entry Point

In the application entry file, the Redux store is created and set to use the root reducer. The store is then passed to all components using the Provider component from the React-Redux helper library.

The `App` root component is rendered on the screen.

```
import React from 'react';
import ReactDOM from 'react-dom';
import { configureStore } from '@reduxjs/toolkit';
import { Provider } from 'react-redux';
import App from './App';

import rootReducer from './rootReducer';

const store = configureStore({
  reducer: rootReducer
```

```
});

ReactDOM.render(
  <React.StrictMode>
  <Provider store={store}>
    <App />
  </Provider>
  </React.StrictMode>,
  document.getElementById('root')
);
```

The store is built using the configureStore helper from the Redux Toolkit. This is similar to creating the store using the createStore function from Redux.

The configureStore adds Redux Thunk as the default library for handling side-effects and turns on the Redux DevTools Extension which helps us debugging the application. It enables us to see all the actions dispatches to the store, check the attached payload data, or view the history of state changes.

Recap

The authentication system involves getting the user credentials and use them to make the login network call and retrieve the authorization token. The token is then saved into the store and used for all the other requests.

The effects encapsulate side-effects like network requests or redirecting the user to another page. They coordinate store updates by dispatching several actions.

All components reading data from the store or dispatching effects must be connected to the store.

Chapter 07: Authorization

Authorization is a security mechanism of granting or denying access to the application features. Our authorization system will give access rights at the page level. All authenticated users will be able to view the secured pages.

At the moment the user can directly access pages like the profile page without being authenticated and authorized. Trying to view the secured pages without being authenticated should redirect the user to the login page.

Private Routes

We can implement such an authorization directly from the routing system. We just need to define some routes as private routes. There is no `PrivateRoute` component in the React Router library, but we can create one using the existing `Route` and `Redirect` components.

```
import React from 'react';
import { Route, Redirect } from 'react-router-dom';

function PrivateRoute ({
    component: Component,
    user,
    ...rest }) {
  return (
    <Route {...rest} render={props => (
    user.authenticated === true
      ? <Component {...props} />
      : <Redirect to='/login' />
  )} />
  )
```

```
}
```

A function can accept all the remaining arguments as an array in the last parameter prefixed with ... and called the rest parameter.

All the props beside the `user` and the `component` received in the rest parameter are sent to the `Route` component using the spread syntax `<Route {...rest} />`.

The `Route` component accepts the `render` prop as a function returning a React element. When the location matches it uses that function to create the React element to be shown.

When the user is authenticated the `PrivateRoute` displays the associated component, otherwise, it redirects the user to the login page.

The `render` prop function has access to all the route props. All these props are send the component using the spread syntax `<Component {...props} />`.

Connect

The `PrivateRoute` component needs to get the current user, so it should be connected to the store.

```
import { connect } from 'react-redux';

function PrivateRoute ({
  component: Component,
  user,
  ...rest }) {}

export default connect(
  ({user}) => ({
    user
  })
)(PrivateRoute);
```

App

Now in the root component, we can just replace `Route` with `PrivateRoute` for all paths that require the user to be authenticated.

Below is an example:

```
<PrivateRoute
 path='/newpost'
 component={NewPost} />
```

Redirect

Once we activate the protected route system, we can notice that the login doesn't work anymore even if the user is actually authenticated. That happens because the `window.location.replace` reloads the new page after the redirect.

After the redirect, the state is restored to the default value so the user is not authenticated anymore.

One solution to this issue is to use the history object from React Router to redirect the user to a new page. This object can be created with the useHistory hook. Once the history object is available it should be sent to the `login` effect.

```
//...
import { useHistory } from "react-router-dom";

function Login({ login }) {

  const history = useHistory();

  function submitForm(){
    const {isValid, errors } = validate();

    if(isValid){
      const credentials = { email, password };
      login(credentials, history);
    } else {
      setErrors(errors);
    }

    //...
  }
}
```

Notice that the `login` callback is called with two arguments, the user credentials and the history object.

Inside the `login` effect, the history object is sent to the `redirectToTimeline` function that uses it to redirect the user to the new page.

```
import api from './api';
import actions from './actions';

function login(credentials, history){
  return function(dispatch){
    return api.login(credentials)
      .then(actions.SetToken)
      .then(dispatch)
      .then(()=>fetchUser(credentials.email))
      .then(dispatch)
      .then(redirectToTimeline(history))
  }
}

function redirectToTimeline(history){
  return function(){
    history.push('/');
  }
}
```

Refresh and Session Storage

Everything seems to be fine now. After the login, the user is redirected to the timeline page. However, if we refresh the page the store is reset to the default value, and the authentication information is lost again.

A solution to this issue is to save the store data in the session storage.

The data in the `sessionStorage` is cleared only when the page session ends. The page session lasts as long as the browser is opened and it persists after a page refresh.

Let's create a new module `sessionStorage.js` with just two functions.

`load` reads the state from session storage. If the state was not previously saved it returns `undefined`.

`save` serializes the state object and saves it in the session storage.

```
function load() {
  const serializedState =
```

```
    sessionStorage.getItem('state');

    return (serializedState !== null)
      ? JSON.parse(serializedState)
      : undefined;
}

function save(state){
  const serializedState =
    JSON.stringify(state);

  sessionStorage
    .setItem('state', serializedState);
}

export default {
  load,
  save
}
```

Now in the `index.js` file, before the store is created we load the previous state from the session storage and pass it to the store.

The `store.subscribe()` method adds a change listener that is called when an action is dispatched. This way we can read the current state object using the `getState()` method and then save it to the session storage.

```
import React from 'react';
import ReactDOM from 'react-dom';
import { configureStore } from '@reduxjs/toolkit';
import { Provider } from 'react-redux';
import App from './App';

import sessionStorage from './shared/sessionStorage';
import rootReducer from './rootReducer';

const persistedState = sessionStorage.load();

const store = configureStore({
  reducer: rootReducer,
  preloadedState: persistedState
```

```
});

store.subscribe(() => {
  const state = store.getState();
  sessionStorage.save(state);
});

ReactDOM.render(
  <React.StrictMode>
    <Provider store={store}>
      <App />
    </Provider>
  </React.StrictMode>,
  document.getElementById('root')
);
```

Recap

A page based authorization system may be enabled using the application router.

The `PrivateRoute` component can be implemented using the existing `Route` and `Redirect` components.

When the page is reloaded the store is reset to its initial value and current user data are lost. We can save the store data in the session storage to avoid losing its data on page refreshes.

Chapter 08: New Post

The New Post page allows the user to create a new blog post.

Let's add behavior to this component.

API

Start by creating the necessary API utility functions.

The `addPost` function creates a new blog post by calling the `/posts` API.

```
import axios from 'axios';
import { header } from '../shared/api';

const baseUrl = 'http://localhost:3001';

function addPost(data, token){
  return axios
    .post(`${baseUrl}/posts`, data,
      header(token));
}

export default {
  addPost
};
```

As you note, accessing the API requires to have an authorization header.

Effects

The `addPost` effect gets information about the current user from the state and creates a new post data object. Then it makes the network call to create the post message and redirects the user to the timeline page.

```
import api from './api';

function addPost(post, history){
  return function(dispatch, getState){
    const state = getState();
    const { user } = state;
    const newPost = {
      ...post,
      userId : user.id,
      userName: user.name
    }

    return api
      .addPost(newPost, user.token)
      .then(redirectToTimeline(history));
  }
}

function redirectToTimeline(history){
  return function(){
    history.push('/')
  }
}

export default {
  addPost
};
```

Now that the state is persisted to the store the `window.location.replace` can also be used to redirect the user to a new page.

```
function addPost(post){
  return function(dispatch, getState){
    //...

    return api
      .addPost(newPost, user.token)
      .then(redirectToTimeline);
  }
}
```

```
function redirectToTimeline(){
  window.location.replace('/');
}
```

New Post Component

The NewPost component has to be connected to the store in order to dispatch the addPost effect.

```
import { connect } from 'react-redux';

function NewPost({ addPost }) {}

export default connect(
  null, {
  ...effects
}
)(NewPost);
```

Recap

The associated logic for the NewPost component turns out to be simple. It just dispatches an effect to add the new blog post and then redirects the user. The timeline page will then reload and display the new post.

Chapter 09: Timeline

Let's continue our journey and develop the logic for the timeline page. The follower's system is not implemented yet so for the moment the timeline page will display all the posts of the current user.

API

The `fetchPosts` function makes a GET network call to retrieve all the posts of a user.

```
import axios from 'axios';
import { getData, header } from '../shared/api';

const baseUrl = 'http://localhost:3001';

function fetchPosts(userId, token){
  return axios
    .get(`${baseUrl}/posts?userId=${userId}`,
      header(token))
    .then(getData);
}
```

The `deletePost` function calls the API to delete a post by id.

```
function deletePost(id, token){
  return axios
    .delete(`${baseUrl}/posts/${id}`,
      header(token));
}
```

State

In order to show the list of people on the screen, we first store this data. The list is initially empty.

```
const initialState = [];
```

Actions

We need just one action to update the current list of blog posts.

```
import { createAction } from '@reduxjs/toolkit';

const SetPosts = createAction('SetPosts');

export default {
  SetPosts
};
```

Effects

The `fetchPosts` effect reads the user's id and token from the store and then makes a network call to retrieve the blog posts. After the result is received from the server it builds the `SetPosts` action and dispatches it to the store.

```
import api from './api';
import actions from './actions';

function fetchPosts(){
  return function(dispatch, getState){
    const state = getState();
    const { user } = state;

    return api
      .fetchPosts(user.id, user.token)
      .then(actions.SetPosts)
      .then(dispatch);
  }
}
```

The `deletePost` effect gets the token from the store and makes the delete API request. Then it builds and dispatches the `fetchPosts` effect that will update the blog posts list.

```
function deletePost(id){
  return function(dispatch, getState){
    const state = getState();
    const { token } = state.user;

    return api
      .deletePost(id, token)
      .then(fetchPosts)
      .then(dispatch)
  }
}
```

Reducer

When the SetPosts action is received the state is updated with the new list of blog posts.

```
import { createReducer } from '@reduxjs/toolkit';
import actions from './actions';

function setPosts(state, action){
  const posts = action.payload;
  return posts;
}

export default createReducer(initialState, {
    [actions.SetPosts]: setPosts
});
```

Root Reducer

We have to update the root reducer to use the new one for managing the list of blog posts.

```
import { combineReducers } from 'redux';
import posts from './posts/reducer';
import user from './user/reducer';

export default combineReducers({
  posts,
```

```
  user
});
```

The combineReducers utility function joins several reducers managing independent parts of the state into the root reducer.

In our case, the `posts` state branch is managed by the `./posts/reducer` and the `user` state branch is managed by the `./user/reducer`.

Timeline Component

The `Timeline` component must be connected to the store to read the list of blog posts and to dispatch the `fetchPosts` and `deletePost` effects.

The `fetchPosts` effect is dispatched when the component is loaded and the `deletePost` effect is dispatched when the delete button is clicked.

```
import React, { useEffect } from 'react';
import { connect } from 'react-redux';
//...

import effects from './effects';
import { getAvatarTitle } from '../user/utils.js';

function Timeline({posts, user, fetchPosts, deletePost}) {

  useEffect(() => {
    fetchPosts();
  },[]);

  return (
  <List>
  {
  posts.map(post => (
    <React.Fragment key={post.id}>
    <!-- ... -->
    {
    (user.id === post.userId) && (
      <ListItemSecondaryAction>
      <IconButton
       onClick={() => deletePost(post.id)}>
        <DeleteIcon />
      </IconButton>
```

```
        </ListItemSecondaryAction>
      )
    }
    <!-- ... -->
    </React.Fragment>
    ))
  }
  </List>
  );
}

export default connect(
  ({posts, user}) => ({
    posts,
    user
  }), {
    ...effects
  }
)(Timeline);
```

Note that conditional rendering is used to display the delete button only when the blog post is created by the current user. When the follower's system is enabled, the blog posts from the followed users will be displayed also.

The `useEffect` hook called with an empty array as the second argument allows executing a callback when the component is loaded.

```
useEffect(() => {
  //...
},[]);
```

App Routes

Make sure you remove all the hardcoded data related to the `Timeline` component from the `App` root component.

```
<PrivateRoute
 path="/"
 exact
 component={Timeline} />
```

Recap

The blog posts have to be saved into the store before being displayed.
The `Timeline` component dispatches an effect to load the blog posts and
update the store with the new list when the page is loaded.

The delete button is displayed only for blog posts created by the current
user using conditional rendering. Clicking the delete button dispatches
the delete blog post effect.

Components must be connected to the store in order to read state data
and dispatch effects.

Chapter 10: People

Next, we will add behavior to the people page. Here the user can see and search for different people.

API

Start by calling the API that can do just that.

fetchOtherUsers makes an API call to retrieve all the users except the current one. If a search text is provided it returns only the users whose names match that text.

```
import axios from 'axios';
import { getData, header } from '../shared/api';

const baseUrl = 'http://localhost:3001';

function fetchOtherUsers(excludedId, text, token){
  const nameQuery =
    text ? `&name_like=${text}` : '';

  return axios
    .get(
      `${baseUrl}/users?id_ne=${excludedId}${nameQuery}`,
      header(token))
    .then(getData);
}

export default {
  fetchOtherUsers
};
```

Again notice that we need to send the authorization token when making the request.

State

We want to display a list of people on the screen so we need this information in the store. The list of people is empty when the application starts.

```
const initialState = [];
```

Actions

We require only one action, SetPeople, to update the state with the new list of people.

```
import { createAction } from '@reduxjs/toolkit';

const SetPeople = createAction('SetPeople');

export default {
  SetPeople
};
```

Effects

The fetchPeople effect reads the current user's id and token from the store and then makes a network call to retrieve the people list based on the provided search text. Then it creates and dispatches the SetPeople action holding the returned list from the server.

```
import api from './api';
import actions from './actions';

function fetchPeople(text){
  return function(dispatch, getState){
    const state = getState();
    const { user } = state;

    return api
      .fetchOtherUsers(user.id, text, user.token)
      .then(actions.SetPeople)
      .then(dispatch);
  }
```

```
}

export default {
  fetchPeople
};
```

Reducer

When the `SetPeople` action is received the state is updated with the new list of people.

```
import { createReducer } from '@reduxjs/toolkit';
import actions from './actions';

const initialState = [];

function setPeople(state, action){
  const people = action.payload;
  return people;
}

export default createReducer(initialState, {
  [actions.SetPeople]: setPeople
});
```

Root Reducer

In the root reducer, we have to make sure that the list of people is managed by the new reducer.

```
import { combineReducers } from 'redux';
import posts from './posts/reducer';
import user from './user/reducer';
import people from './people/peopleReducer';

export default combineReducers({
  posts,
  user,
  people
});
```

People Component

The People component should be connected to the store to read the list of people and dispatch the fetchPeople effect when the component loads or when the search button is clicked.

```
import React, { useEffect } from 'react';
import { connect } from 'react-redux';

import PeopleSearch from './PeopleSearch';
import PeopleList from './PeopleList';

import effects from './effects';

function People({people, fetchPeople}) {

  useEffect(() => {
    fetchPeople();
  },[]);

  return (
    <React.Fragment>
      <PeopleSearch
       onSearch={fetchPeople}
      />

      <PeopleList
       people={people}
      />
    </React.Fragment>
  );
}

export default connect(
  ({people}) => ({
      people
  }), {
    ...effects
  }
)(People);
```

App

Don't forget to clear all the hardcoded data passed to the `People` component from the `App` root component.

```
<PrivateRoute
 path="/people"
 component={People} />
```

Recap

The `People` component first loads the people by dispatching a fetch effect. The list of people is saved in the store and then displayed on the screen.

When the search button is clicked the same fetch effect is dispatched but this time with a search text. The network call is made again to retrieved the list of people and the store is updated by dispatching an action. When the state branch has updated the `People` component using it is rerendered

Chapter 11: Follow

Next, we are going to implement the follow/unfollow feature.

API

Start by defining the required API calls.

The `addFollower` function makes a network call to add a new following relation. The data object contains two properties: `userId` and `followerId`.

```
import axios from 'axios';
import { getData, getFirst, header }
  from '../shared/api';

const baseUrl = 'http://localhost:3001';

function addFollower(data, token){
  return axios
    .post(`${baseUrl}/followers`, data,
      header(token));
}
```

The `deleteFollowingItem` function makes a network call to delete the following relation by id.

```
function deleteFollowingItem(id, token){
  return axios
    .delete(`${baseUrl}/followers/${id}`,
      header(token));
}
```

The fake API allows us to delete the following relations only by their ids. In case we don't have these ids we can search for them using the `fetchFollowingItem` API utility function that retrieves a relation by `userId` and `followerId`.

```
function fetchFollowingItem(userId, followerId, token){
  return axios
    .get(
`${baseUrl}/followers?userId=${userId}&followerId=${followerId}`,
  header(token))
    .then(getData)
    .then(getFirst);
}
```

The `fetchFollowing` makes the API call to retrieve the ids of the followed users.

```
function fetchFollowing(userId, token){
  return axios
    .get(
      `${baseUrl}/followers?followerId=${userId}`,
      header(token))
    .then(getData)
}
```

The `fetchUsersByIds` makes the network call to get users by their ids. It can be used for example after we have the ids of the followed users.

```
function fetchUsersByIds(ids, token){
  const query = ids.length
    ? `&id=${ids.join('&id=')}`
    : ''

  return axios
    .get(`${baseUrl}/users?${query}`,
      header(token))
    .then(getData);
}
```

State

We need to store the list of the followed users in order to show it on screen. The list is initially empty.

```
const initialState = [];
```

Actions

An action for updating the state with the new list of the followed users is required.

```
import { createAction } from '@reduxjs/toolkit';

const SetFollowingList = createAction('SetFollowingList');
```

Effects

The fetchFollowing effect gets the current user's id and token from the store. It then makes a call to retrieve the followed users' relation objects. After that, it converts this list of relation objects into a list of user ids using the extractProp utility. The list of ids is then used to retrieve the list of people. The returned list is utilized to create and dispatch the SetFollowingList action for updating the store.

```
import api from './api';
import actions from './actions';

function fetchFollowing(){
  return function(dispatch, getState){
    const state = getState();
    const { user } = state;

    return api
      .fetchFollowing(user.id, user.token)
      .then(extractProp('userId'))
      .then(fetchPeopleByIds(user.token))
      .then(actions.SetFollowingList)
      .then(dispatch);
  }
}
```

The fetchPeopleByIds utility function makes a network call to retrieved a list of users based on their ids. It is a curried function. It first takes a token and returns a function that gets the list of ids.

```
function fetchPeopleByIds(token){
  return function(ids){
    return ids.length
      ? api.fetchUsersByIds(ids, token)
```

```
    : Promise.resolve([]);
  }
}
```

The **prop** utility returns the value of the specified property name from an object. It is a curried function. It gets the property name and returns a function taking the object.

```
function prop(propName){
  return function(obj){
    return obj[propName];
  }
}
```

The **extractProp** uses the **prop** function to create a list containing only the values of the specified property name.

```
function extractProp(propName){
  return function(list){
    return list.map(prop(propName));
  }
}
```

The **follow** effect reads the current user from the store and then makes the network call to create the following relation. Then it builds and dispatches the **fetchFollowing** effect that updates the store with the new list of followed users.

```
function follow(userId){
  return function(dispatch, getState){
    const state = getState();
    const { user } = state;
    const newFollower = {
      userId,
      followerId: user.id
    }

    return api
      .addFollower(newFollower, user.token)
      .then(fetchFollowing)
      .then(dispatch);
  }
}
```

The unfollow effect gets the current user from the store and then makes a network call to retrieve the relation object. Then it calls the deleteFollowingBy utility that extracts the relation id and does the network call to delete that following relation. After that, it builds and dispatches the fetchFollowing effect that updates the store with the new list of followed users.

```
function unfollow(userId){
  return function(dispatch, getState){
    const state = getState();
    const { user } = state;

    return api
      .fetchFollowingItem(userId, user.id, user.token)
      .then(deleteFollowingBy(user.token))
      .then(fetchFollowing)
      .then(dispatch)
  }
}
```

The deleteFollowingBy deletes the following relation by id. It is a curried function. First, it takes a token and returns a function that takes the id.

```
function deleteFollowingBy(token){
  return function({id}){
    return api.deleteFollowingItem(id, token)
  }
}
```

Timeline Effects

The fetchPosts effect, used to update the current list of blog posts displayed on the timeline page, needs to take into consideration the list of followed users.

fetchPosts reads the list of followed users from the store and transforms it into a simple list of ids that is then sent to the fetch API utility function.

```
import api from './api';
import actions from './actions';


function fetchPosts(){
```

```
  return function(dispatch, getState){
    const state = getState();
    const { user, followingList } = state;
    const followingIds =
      followingList.map(x => x.id);

    return api
      .fetchPosts(user.id, followingIds, user.token)
      .then(actions.SetPosts)
      .then(dispatch);
  }
}
```

fetchPosts API utility uses the list of users' ids to build a query string
with all the user's ids for whom to retrieve the blog posts.

```
function fetchPosts(userId, followingIds, token){
  const followingRequest = followingIds.length
    ? `&userId=${followingIds.join('&userId=')}`
    : ''

  return axios.get(
    `${baseUrl}/posts?userId=${userId}${followingRequest}`,
    header(token))
    .then(getData);
}
```

Reducer

When the SetFollowingList action is received the store is updated with
the new list of followed users.

```
import { createReducer } from '@reduxjs/toolkit';
import actions from '../actions';

function setFollowingList(state, action){
  const list = action.payload;
  return list;
}

export default createReducer(initialState, {
  [actions.SetFollowingList]: setFollowingList
```

```
});
```

Root Reducer

We must update the root reducer to use the new reducer managing the followed users.

```
import { combineReducers } from 'redux';
import posts from './posts/reducer';
import user from './user/reducer';
import people from './people/reducers/peopleReducer';
import followingList from './people/reducers/followingReducer';

export default combineReducers({
  posts,
  user,
  people,
  followingList
});
```

PeopleList Component

Then PeopleList component needs to be connected to the store to have access to the follow and unfollow effects. It also requires access to a map with the followed users in order to display correctly the follow and unfollow buttons.

```
import React from 'react';
import { connect } from 'react-redux';

//...

import { getAvatarTitle } from '../user/utils.js';
import { createMapById } from '../shared/map';
import effects from './effects';

function PeopleList({people, followingMap, follow, unfollow}) {

return (
  <List>
  {
    people.map(user => (
```

```
    <ListItem key={user.id}>
      <ListItemAvatar>
      <Avatar alt={user.name}>
        {getAvatarTitle(user.name)}
      </Avatar>
      </ListItemAvatar>
      <ListItemText
       primary={user.name}
      />
      <ListItemSecondaryAction>
      { followingMap.has(user.id)
        ? <IconButton
          onClick={() => unfollow(user.id)}>
          <PersonAddDisabledIcon />
          </IconButton>
        : <IconButton
          onClick={() => follow(user.id)}>
          <PersonAddIcon />
          </IconButton>
      }
      </ListItemSecondaryAction>
    </ListItem>
    ))
  }
  </List>
  );
}


export default connect(
  ({followingList}) => ({
      followingMap : createMapById(followingList)
  }), {
    ...effects
  }
)(PeopleList);
```

Note that `PeopleList` checks the user's id in the followed users map. Based on that it uses conditional rendering to display the follow or the unfollow buttons.

`createMapById` is a utility function that creates a new map from a list using the id property as the key and the object itself as the value.

```
function createMapById(list){
  const map = new Map();

  list.forEach(user => {
    map.set(user.id, user);
  });

  return map;
}
```

Recap

The `PeopleList` displays the lists of people received in the input props. It is connected to the store in order to dispatch the follow and unfollow effects when the user clicks the specific button.

When the follow button is clicked, the follow effect is dispatched to add a new following relation. Then the list of followed users is updated by dispatching an action to the store. This list update results in the display of the unfollow button on the screen.

When the unfollow button is press, the unfollow effect is dispatched. Then the store is updated with the new list of followed users, which in turn results in the display of the follow button on the screen for that person.

Chapter 12: Profile

The profile page displays information about the current user including the list of followed users and all the followers.

We already have all the followed users so next, we need to make sure that we also have all the followers.

Let's start.

API

`fetchFollowers` makes a network call to retrieve all followers for a user.

```
import axios from 'axios';
import { getData } from '../shared/api';

function fetchFollowers(userId, token){
  return axios
    .get(
    `${baseUrl}/followers?userId=${userId}`,
      header(token))
    .then(getData)
}
```

State

We must store the list of followers to then display it on screen. It will be initially empty.

```
const initialState = [];
```

Actions

We require a new action for updating the followers' list in the store.

```
import { createAction } from '@reduxjs/toolkit';

const SetFollowersList = createAction('SetFollowersList');
```

Effects

The `fetchFollowers` effect reads the user's id and token from the store. Then it calls the `fetchFollowers` API utility to get all the follower's relational objects. It extracts the user ids and uses them to get all these users in full details. After that, it builds the `SetFollowersList` action and dispatches it to the store.

```
import api from './api';
import actions from './actions';

function fetchFollowers(){
  return function(dispatch, getState){
    const state = getState();
    const { user } = state;

    return api
      .fetchFollowers(user.id, user.token)
      .then(extractProp('followerId'))
      .then(fetchPeopleByIds(user.token))
      .then(actions.SetFollowersList)
      .then(dispatch);
  }
}
```

Reducer

When the `SetFollowersList` is dispatched the reducer updates the follower's list with the new value.

```
import { createReducer } from '@reduxjs/toolkit';
import actions from '../actions';

const initialState = [];
```

```
function setFollowersList(state, action){
  const list = action.payload;
  return list;
}


export default createReducer(initialState, {
  [actions.SetFollowersList]: setFollowersList
});
```

Root Reducer

We need to update the root reducer to manage the follower's list using the new reducer.

```
import { combineReducers } from 'redux';
import posts from './posts/reducer';
import user from './user/reducer';
import people from
  './people/reducers/peopleReducer';
import followingList from
  './people/reducers/followingReducer';
import followersList from
  './people/reducers/followersReducer';

export default combineReducers({
  posts,
  user,
  people,
  followingList,
  followersList
});
```

People Component

The `People` component has to be connected to the store to read the information about the current user, the list of followers, and the list of followed users. It also needs access to the `fetchFollowing` and `fetchFollowers` effects that are dispatched when the component is loaded.

```
import React, { useEffect } from 'react';
import { connect } from 'react-redux';
//...
```

```
import effects from './effects';

function People({
    user, followingList, followersList,
    fetchFollowing, fetchFollowers}) {

  useEffect(() => {
    fetchFollowing();
    fetchFollowers();
  },[]);

  //...
}

export default connect(
  ({user, followingList, followersList}) => ({
      user,
      followingList,
      followersList
  }), {
    ...effects
  }
)(People);
```

App

Don't forget to remove all hardcoded data sent to the `Profile` component in the `App` root when defining the routes.

```
<PrivateRoute
 path="/profile"
 component={Profile} />
```

Recap

The `Profile` component dispatches two effects when the component is loaded to fetch both the list of followers and the followed users. The results from the server are then used to build actions for updating the store with the new lists. When the store is updated the `Profile` component is re-rendered.

Chapter 13: Server Errors

In the next chapter, we will look at catching and displaying the server error. For this, we will create a new helper module that can render this kind of errors.

State

We should have two pieces of information regarding the server error, the error message, and a boolean indicating if it should be displayed. The user will be allowed to hide the server error.

```
const initialState = {
  serverError : '',
  showError: false
}
```

Actions

We need two actions one for updating the error message and another one for hiding the error message already displayed on the screen.

```
import { createAction } from '@reduxjs/toolkit';

const ShowServerError = createAction('SetServerError');
const HideServerError = createAction('HideServerError');

export default {
  ShowServerError,
  HideServerError
};
```

Reducer

When the `ShowServerError` action is dispatched the associated reducer will update the error message and mark it to be shown on screen.

When the `HideServerError` action is dispatched the associated reducer will mark the error message as not to be displayed on the screen.

```
import { createReducer } from '@reduxjs/toolkit';
import actions from './actions';

function showServerError(state, action){
  const error = action.payload;
  const serverError = error.response
   ? error.response.data
   : error.message;

  return {
    ...state,
    serverError,
    showError: true
  };
}

function hideServerError(state, action){
  return {
    ...state,
    showError: false
  };
}

export default createReducer(initialState, {
  [actions.ShowServerError]: showServerError,
  [actions.HideServerError]: hideServerError
});
```

Root Reducer

In the end, we need to update the root reducer to use the new reducer for the server error management.

```
import { combineReducers } from 'redux';
import posts from './posts/reducer';
```

```
import user from './user/reducer';
import people from './people/reducers/peopleReducer';
import followingList from './people/reducers/followingReducer';
import followersList from './people/reducers/followersReducer';
import network from './network/reducer';

export default combineReducers({
  posts,
  user,
  people,
  followingList,
  followersList,
  network
});
```

Component

Next, let's build the **ServerError** component that reads the error message from the store and displays it on screen.

```
import React from 'react';
import Container from
  '@material-ui/core/Container';
import Alert from
  '@material-ui/lab/Alert';
import Box from
  '@material-ui/core/Box';

import actions from './actions';
import { connect } from 'react-redux';

function ServerError({
    showError,
    serverError,
    HideServerError }) {
  return showError
    ? <Container maxWidth="xs">
        <Box mb={1} mt={1}>
          <Alert
            severity="error"
            onClose={HideServerError}>
```

```
                {serverError}
              </Alert>
            </Box>
          </Container>
        : (null);
}


export default connect(
  ({ network }) => ({
    serverError: network.serverError,
    showError: network.showError
  }),{
    ...actions
  }
)(ServerError);
```

Root Component

The new **ServerError** component should be used in the **App** root component, so we can see the server error message on all pages.

```
import React from 'react';
import { BrowserRouter as Router, Route, Switch }
    from 'react-router-dom';

import ServerError from './network/ServerError';

function App() {
  return (
    <Router>
      <!-- -->
      <ServerError />
    </Router>
  );
}


export default App;
```

Login Effect

Let's now update the `login` effect to display the server error message when an error is received from the server. We simply add a `catch` close to handle the error by creating and dispatching the `ShowServerError` action.

```
.catch(networkActions.ShowServerError)
.then(dispatch);
```

Here is how the updated login effect looks like.

```
import api from './api';
import actions from './actions';
import networkActions from '../network/actions';
import peopleEffects from '../people/effects';

function login(credentials){
  return function(dispatch){
    return api.login(credentials)
      .then(actions.SetToken)
      .then(dispatch)
      .then(()=>fetchUser(credentials.email))
      .then(dispatch)
      .then(peopleEffects.fetchFollowing)
      .then(dispatch)
      .then(redirectToTimeline)
      .catch(networkActions.ShowServerError)
      .then(dispatch);
  }
}
```

Recap

We can encapsulate the server error handling inside a shared module. This module has a component for displaying the error message in a panel that can be closed by dispatching an action.

Inside the other effect functions, we need to handle the errors on API calls by creating and dispatching a server error action with the new error message.

Chapter 14: Review

When we look back at how the application was implemented we noticed that we followed the unidirectional data flow paradigm and split its main parts into smaller pieces.

The other thing one can remark is that we followed the functional principles of aiming for pure functions, respecting immutability, and expressing data transformations using pipelines.

State Tree

In order to better manage the state in our application, we had to split it into parts.

```
|-posts
|-user
   -token
   -id
   -name
   -email
   -authenticated
|-people
|-followingList
|-followersList
|-network
  -serverError
  -showError
```

The state management of these state branches was also split between different reducers. This can be clearly seen in the `rootReducer.js` file.

```
import { combineReducers } from 'redux';
import posts from './posts/reducer';
```

```
import user from './user/reducer';
import people from
    './people/reducers/peopleReducer';
import followingList from
    './people/reducers/followingReducer';
import followersList from
    './people/reducers/followersReducer';
import network from './network/reducer';

export default combineReducers({
    posts,
    user,
    people,
    followingList,
    followersList,
    network
});
```

For example the `./posts/reducer` is responsible for managing the `posts` branch, the `./user/reducer` reducer manages the `user` branch and so on.

Component Tree

In order to better understand and manage the UI we split into parts. We ended up with a component tree.

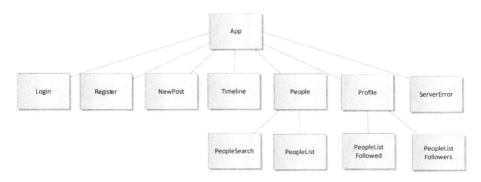

Folder Structure

When organizing the application files I suggest taking a feature-first approach. That means first grouping the files by the feature they belong to and then group them by their type.

Here is an example.

```
posts/
  |-- actions.js
  |-- reducer.js
  |-- api.js
  |-- effects.js
  |-- NewPost.jsx
  |-- Timeline.jsx
people/
  |-- actions.js
  |-- reducer.js
  |-- api.js
  |-- effects.js
  |-- reducers/
      |-- followerReducer.js
      |-- followingReducer.js
      |-- peopleReducer.js
      |-- ...
  |-- People.jsx
  |-- PeopleList.jsx
  |-- PeopleSearch.jsx
  |-- Profile.jsx
  |--...
```

Inside the `people` folder, we can group further the components in their own folder.

Immutability

We can simply impose immutability on our application using a linter. ESLint comes already with Create React App so we just need to install an additional plugin like eslint-plugin-immutable to impose immutable objects.

```
npm install eslint-plugin-immutable --save-dev
```

Here is the plugin configuration inside the `.eslintrc` file.

```
{
  "extends": ["react-app"],
  "plugins": [
```

```
      "immutable"
   ],
   "rules": {
      "immutable/no-this": "error",
      "immutable/no-mutation": "error"
   }
}
```

Purity

In functional programming, the main focus is to work with pure functions. Sadly for us there is no popular library for React that allows us to work only with pure functions. However, by using Redux for state management we manage to improve the purity of our application.

Several function components were pure. All reducer functions were pure.

Side-effects were encapsulated mainly in the effect functions. In components, the side-effects were wrapped inside the `useEffect` hook.

Pipelines

When you look back, you can see that effect functions were implemented using pipelines.

```
function fetchFollowers(){
   return function(dispatch, getState){
      const state = getState();
      const { user } = state;

      return api
         .fetchFollowers(user.id, user.token)
         .then(extractProp('followerId'))
         .then(fetchPeopleByIds(user.token))
         .then(actions.SetFollowersList)
         .then(dispatch);
   }
}

function fetchPeopleByIds(token){}
function prop(propName){}
function extractProp(propName){}
```

Here is how this pipeline looks like. Notice how the output of one function is used as input for the next one.

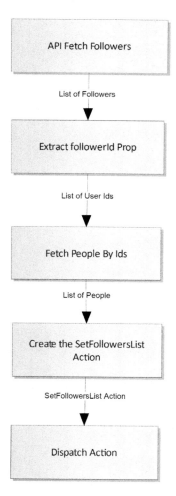

Recap

The concept of modularity, of splitting things into parts for better management can be seen not only at the UI level where the page is split into components but also when managing state. The state is split into branches each managed by a specific reducer.

Our aim was to build pure functions transforming immutable data and trying to make these transformations more expressive using pipelines.

What's next?

For a more in-depth look at JavaScript and main functional principles, you may read 'Discover Functional JavaScript'. Here, you will find more on pure functions, immutability, currying, decorators but also ideas on how to make code easier to read. JavaScript brings functional programming to the mainstream and offers a new way of doing object-oriented programming without classes and prototypes.

In the 'Functional Programming in JavaScript' book you will find how to use JavaScript as a functional programming language by disabling the 'this' keyword and enforcing immutable objects with a linter. You will learn how to use statements like 'if' and 'switch' in a functional way, or how to create and use functors and monads. It turns out that JavaScript has everything it needs to be used as a functional language. We just have to remove features from the language.

If you want to learn how to build modern React applications using functional components and functional programming principles, you can consider reading 'Functional React, 2nd Edition'.

Functional Architecture
with React and Redux

Cristian Salcescu

Continue your learning path with 'Functional Architecture with React and Redux' book, and put in practice what you learned by building several applications with an incremental level of complexity.

The functional architecture implies getting the initial state, showing it to the user using the view functions, listening for actions, updating the state based on those actions, and rendering the updated state back to the user again.

UI State Management
From Object-Oriented to Functional

Cristian Salcescu

The 'UI State Management' book gives you an overview of how state is managed by building a note-taking application with four different libraries. We start from an object-oriented approach using Svelte, centralize state with Vuex, then move to a functional approach with React and Redux, and in the end arrive at a solution using only pure functions with Elm.

Vue.js
Composition API

Cristian Salcescu

The Composition API provides a new way of managing reactivity. It is made of a set of Reactive API functions plus the facility to register lifecycle hooks. Understand better the reactivity system by building one from scratch and then implement a master-details functionality. Check how to manage state using the Composition API and then use it to implement a central store similar to Vuex.

Enjoy the learning journey!

About the author

Cristian Salcescu is the author of Functional React.

He is a Technical Lead passionate about front-end development and enthusiastic about sharing ideas. He took different roles and participated in all parts of software creation.

Cristian Salcescu is a JavaScript trainer and a writer on Medium.